JAPANESE FLOWER ARRANGEMENT
in a Nutshell

Japanese Flower Arrangement in a Nutshell

A Primer

ELLEN GORDON ALLEN

CHARLES E. TUTTLE COMPANY
Rutland, Vermont & Tokyo, Japan

Representatives
Continental Europe: Boxerbooks, Inc., *Zurich*
British Isles: Prentice-hall International, Inc., *London*
Australasia: Book Wise (Australia) Pty. Ltd.
104-108 Sussex Street, Sydney 2000

Published by the Charles E. Tuttle Company
of Rutland, Vermont and Tokyo, Japan
with editorial offices at
Suido 1-chome, 2-6 Bunkyo-ku, Tokyo

Copyright in Japan, 1955 by Charles E. Tuttle Co., Inc.

International Standard Book No. 0-8048-0295-5

First printing, 1955
Twenty-ninth printing, 1986

PRINTED IN JAPAN

*This little book is dedicated to the
Great Masters of Japanese Flower Arrangement
who through their genius have so enriched our lives*

Table of Contents

Foreword

It was with great pleasure that I learned that the art of Japanese flower arrangement has been introduced into the United States and is being warmly received there.

Mrs. Ellen G. Allen is a most suitable interpreter of flower arrangement to the American public. While in Japan, she studied with diligence and enthusiasn the principles of both the classical and modern schools.

Unfortunately, some students of flower arrangement mistakenly believe that once they have studied one of the many various schools, they have mastered all the secrets of Japanese flower arrangement. In contrast to this, the thorough training which Mrs. Allen has received leads me to lend my wholehearted endorsement to her book, with its wide and objective treatment of the entire field.

It is a matter of pride and joy for me to have taught Mrs. Allen and to have awarded her the diploma of my school, thus making her the first qualified teacher of the Ohara School in the United States since I became Headmaster.

I congratulate Mrs. Allen on her success in compiling this excellent outline of Japanese flower arrangement. I particularly recommend it to those in America who wish to know the correct fundamentals of the Ohara School.

February 14, 1954

Houn Ohara, Headmaster
Ohara School of
Japanese Flower Arrangement

Introduction

There is something of the artist in each of us. Some find expression in painting, some in poetry, some in sculpture, some in landscaping and others in a variety of ways.

With talent, expression of these art forms is satisfying. Seldom, however, is found a person talented in all of the media mentioned. It may be a new realization to the reader, then, to find that here is an art (an ancient one) that can express a thought, a mood, combining the best of other media. Particular talent in flower arranging is not essential. The "feeling" is engendered by practice.

The purpose of this primer is to acquaint the reader with elementary knowledge in a special school of flower arranging—the Japanese school—selected because it is the oldest and its teachings are perhaps the simplest, yet most effective.

The text is intended for amateurs, but professional arrangers might find it useful as a refresher. The author is indebted to Mr. Houn Ohara and his volume, "Japanese Flower Arrangement," for much of the material included here.

Why This Primer?

I cannot begin this primer without paying tribute to my first class in Japanese Flower Arrangement in the United States. It is to these students and their insistence that I write up my lectures that this primer came into being. Nor can I forget my former classmates who studied flower arrangement with me in Japan and who, through the medium of this art, became close friends.

Principal purpose behind the writing of this primer on Japanese Flower Arrangement was two-fold:

First, many of my students desired a more comprehensive understanding of the art, particularly something to help them when no teacher would be available.

Second, it was written for all people who love flowers and love to arrange them — and all who want to learn the art of Japanese Flower Arrangement.

It is my hope that this primer will serve as a practical handbook for the beginner. To achieve that end, I have made my directions and explanations as elementary, practical, detailed and direct to the point as possible.

I have eliminated as much as possible all Japanese terms, substituting English equivalents. The few fundamental rules which form the basis for Japanese Flower Arrangement and the various techniques have been outlined and listed in a manner which I hope is simplified and understandable.

Each lesson is detailed with steps and accompanying sketches which clearly show what should be done as the arrangement progresses towards completion.

Using this step-by-step method should enable you to learn rapidly while enjoying your progress. It is the enjoyment of flower arrangement that I want to stress. Learn the fundamentals well and you will share your great enjoyment with others who will marvel at your skill in flower arrangement.

So, let's have fun!

Basic Information

Before beginning these lessons in the elementary instruction of Japanese Flower Arrangement, it is necessary to become familiar with certain basic information relative to the mechanics of flower arrangements and the terminology used in these instructions. Japanese terms will be used sparingly, only where absolutely necessary.

There are two fundamental basic styles or designs of Japanese Flower Arrangement. Each is identified by the type of container used. Moribana is the style which uses the open-mouth low bowl or horizontal container. Best translation of the word seems to be "flowers arranged in a horizontal container or bowl in which is placed a holder set in a fixed position." Heika applies to arrangements which use the perpendicular vase and, freely translated, means "flowers arranged in a vase in such a manner that they seem to be thrown into the vase." This translation may be misleading since, although the flowers may have the appearance of "being thrown" into the vase, actually, as we will find out in our lessons, each flower, branch, and shrub is placed in a certain position in the vase with great care, following the rules for this style of arrangement. No metal holder is used in the Heika arrangement.

The Moribana and Heika styles or designs are further divided into three "forms" which will be called forms "A," "B," and "C." The difference in the placement of the three principal stems determines whether the arrangr follows Form "A" (upright), Form "B" (slanting forward) or Form "C" (slanting sideways). Two additional styles of Japanese Flower Arrangement, although not basic ones, will be presented and explained in the lessons which follow. Although a Form "D" is included in the Ohara School for the Moribana style arrangement, I am not going to develop it in this primer, since it is not practical for use in our Western homes. Instead we will designate the water reflecting or natural scenery arrangements as Form "D" in the Moribana arrangements. In the Heika arrangements, Form "D" will be devoted to the "cascade."

Since Japanese Flower Arrangement is basically concerned with the arrangement of the three principal flowers or stems, regardless of what form or style is used, it is up to the beginner to learn the correct positions of these principal stems. Additional flowers may be added to each arrangement, but the correct positions of the principal stems are of major importance.

The three principal stems are the subject stem, the secondary stem and the object stem. In the lessons which follow, these principal stems will be designated by the same name, regardless of what style or form of arrangement is being outlined. All additional material used in a flower arrangement will be called fillers. Intermediary is the official name of the "filler" according to the Ohara School, but I prefer to use "filler" and will describe these additional stems as fillers in the lessons which follow.

One of the most difficult problems confronting Americans in regard to Japanese styles of arrangements, and one which frequently proves to be a stumbling block for beginners, is the various combinations of materials that may be used to complete the various styles and forms of arrangements. In one arrangement, each principal stem may be a flower or flowers. Another arrangement might have a flower or flowers for the subject and secondary stems, with a shrub or small branches used for the object stem. A third variation might have a branch or shrub for the subject and secondary stems with a flower or flowers making up the object stem. A flower or flowers may be used for the subject stem with shrubs or branches making up the secondary and object stems. All of this material is cut according to the respective measurement rules and the same material used for principal stems may be repeated for the fillers. Whatever combinations are used, however, no more than three different materials may be used in any one arrangement.

Basic measurement rules for lengths of principal stems and fillers have been developed for both the Moribana and Heika styles and these rules will be followed in this primer exactly as given here. Two rules will be given for the Moribana style while the Heika style uses one basic rule.

Rule I — For Moribana style arrangements:

If round container is used: For subject stem, measure diameter of container then add depth in inches. Thus, if the container is 10 inches in diameter and two inches deep, the subject stem will measure 12 inches in length. Secondary stem measures two-thirds of subject stem. If subject stem measures 12 inches, then secondary stem would be eight inches long. Object stem measures one-half length of subject stem, making object stem six inches long, if a 12 inch subject stem is used. This rule may also apply to oblong or rectangular containers, and this adaptation was used in the sketches accompanying the Moribana Lessons in this primer.

Rule II — For Moribana style arrangements:

If oblong container is used: Subject stem will measure 1½ times length of oblong container. If container 10 inches long is used, subject stem would measure 15 inches. Secondary stem is two-thirds length of subject stem or 10 inches in this case. Object stem is one-half length of subject stem or 7½ inches if we use a 15 inch subject stem.

In some cases, depending upon the container and materials used, Rule II is modified and the depth of the container is used in measuring length of the three principal stems. Thus, for subject stem, length would be 1½ times length of container, plus depth. If container measures 10 inches long by two inches deep, subject stem would be 17 inches in length. Secondary and object stems would maintain regular relationship to subject stem, as outlined in Rule I.*

Rule III — For Heika style arrangements:

Subject stem: 1½ times height of vase. If vase is 10 inches high, subject stem would measure 15 inches. Secondary stem: two-thirds length of subject stem or 10 inches in length, if a 15-inch subject stem is being used. Object stem: one-half of subject stem or 7½ inches if a 15-inch subject stem is used. These basic measurement rules never vary.

* The selection of the Moribana rule by the beginner depends upon the material to be arranged and the placement of the finished arrangement.

In the lessons which follow, the student must be thoroughly familiar with them.

Regarding proportions among the three principal stems, although the orthodox measurement rules just outlined never vary, naturally some adjustment in length of subject stem must be made if the flower or branch to be used is not long enough. Select a subject stem which comes closest to the proper length, then measure the secondary and object stems in proportion to the subject stem. This difficulty of having to utilize a too-short subject stem occurred in preparing the arrangement illustrating Lesson 2. To offset this, the holder was placed close to the front of the container, to "elongate" the arrangement as far as the eyes and the subject stem were concerned. In Lesson 3, the same thing happened when the rose stems were not long enough. To overcome this difficulty, the holder was placed just off center, giving the impression of a longer stem.

Rule for fillers:

Filler 1 is cut two-thirds length of secondary stem. Filler 2 is cut one-half length of Filler 1. Filler 3 is cut either shorter or longer than Filler 2, depending upon whichever size fits better into the completed arrangement.

Position of fillers in the completed arrangement is left to the discretion of the arranger. Object is to use fillers to make the completed arrangement beautiful, filled out and finished in appearance. Common sense is the best guide here.

No accurate and fool-proof measurement rule can be laid down for material used as fillers. Flowers, branches, etc., vary, both in shape and number of leaves on stems. These factors influence the use of fillers. To aid the student, a basic measurement rule has been devised for fillers and will be followed in this primer.

It is practically impossible to add length to stems of flowers, shrubs, and branches used in Moribana style of arrangements, but in the Heika (or Nageire),* stems may be easily elongated by utilizing any of the artificial methods presented in Lesson 5, and the measurement rule for Heika arrangements may be followed accurately. Common sense will guide the student when problems of this nature occur, and the beginner must remember as she progresses that a flower arrangement is supposed to look beautiful, as well as follow the rules.

Two types of holders will be used in the Moribana style lessons, the open-type holder and the needle point holder. In the open-type holder, the three principal parts will be called sections.

The needle point holder, the type most commonly available and used in this country, will be separated into four divisions, 1-2-3-4. In explaining the use of the needle type holder, these numbered divisions will be of great importance. In the diagrams which accompany and illustrate each lesson, solid lines will denote the principal stems and broken lines will indicate fillers.

* Both Heika and Nageire refer to identical style.

8

Before attempting the first lesson, the reader should be certain to have a firm grasp of the essentials listed above. These essentials are basic to all Japanese flower arranging. In these lessons on elementary Japanese Flower Arrangement, which follow, diagrams will be used whenever necessary.

Although I am teaching principally the methods of Japanese Flower Arrangement as taught by the Ohara School, this primer also contains additional information learned from other schools. I have tried to present in this primer over-all information concerning the art, and particularly that which I consider essential and practical for our use in America.

Pictures of Japanese free style or advanced Japanese Flower Arrangement have been included in this book to help train the eye of the student for advance work. Since I am endeavoring to stress as strongly as possible, the designs of Japanese flower arrangement and the variety of combinations of flowers, foliage, shrubs, etc., that may be used, these pictures will show what can be accomplished once preliminary instruction has been completed. Free style arrangements will automatically develop as a result of a good foundation, coupled with continual practice.

High cost of color printing has prevented the reproduction of the flower arrangements pictured in this primer in full color. Although personally disappointing, the elimination of color plates has enabled the authoress to keep the price of the finished primer as low as possible. Despite this lack of color, the "design" which is absolutely basic in all Japanese flower arrangements is very evident in the black and white reproductions. A definite design is pre-eminently evident in all the pictures used, regardless of whether examples of basic, advanced or free style arrangements are depicted.

Before beginning the first lesson, let me assure you that Japanese Flower Arrangement is extremely easy and simple to learn. It may at first appear to be difficult and complex, but it is no different than learning other forms of art.

To those who overcome the obstacles confronting any beginner and persevere, eventual mastery of Japanese Flower Arrangement will be your reward. Therefore, be patient, persevere and work hard and a new field of beauty will unfold under your accomplished hands.

Preliminary

Like any other art — painting, sculpture, music, even cooking — a certain amount of equipment is essential for the study of Japanese Flower Arrangement. The arrangements to be explained and outlined in this primer will require only the simplest of items, but they are essential equipment. At least six articles are required:

One horizontal container or low bowl.

One perpendicular container or vase.

Clippers.

Holders, both metal open-type holder and a needle-point holder.

Wire or string.

Basket or tin box.

Containers

In flower arranging, the term **container** is often used. It applies to two types: the horizontal, open-mouthed **low bowl,** and the perpendicular or upright container, which will be referred to from now on as a **vase.**

Heika Vase

Since the low bowl and the vase may be of any size, shape, material, color, etc., the important factor is the adaptability of the container to its use in the arrangements. Beginners should have one medium-sized low bowl and one medium-sized vase. For variety, I recommend a white low bowl and a green, yellow or gray vase, since these colors blend most successfully with flowers

Moribana Low Bowl

Holders

The metal holder is one of the most important items used in Japanese Flower Arrangements. It is a molded form, made of lead, with open sections which are designed in such a way that stems may be placed in the open sections to secure them in position. You may readily identify this holder as a "frog."

The Ohara School, as do many Japanese schools of flower arrangement, considers this open type holder preferable to the common pin type or needle holder, so popular in this country. One advantage of the open type holder is that it is designed so that the flower, branch, shrub or foliage remains securely where placed, since the tip of the stem is cut to fit in the section of the holder. Also, the stem is always submerged in water, because the bottom of this type of holder is open and placed

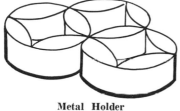

directly on the bottom of the container. The needle point holder is not open on the bottom and frequently, if the container is shallow, the stems in the needle point holders are above the water level.

Metal Holder

In addition, the open-type holder permits the arranger to prevent stems and fillers from wobbling or falling once they have been correctly cut and placed in proper position. A flower stem that is too small

to fit tightly in the opening can be secured by cutting small sticks, or taking left-over parts of stems from material at hand and using these "cuttings" to serve as wedges to secure the flowers, branches, or shrubs.

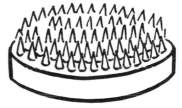

Needle Point Holder

The needle point holder is a heavy, rounded or oblong metal block from which extends sharp points, like needles. These needles are used to spear the stems of the flowers and hold them in the proper positions in the container. This type of holder is very practical when using flowers with thick, soft stems, but it is not easy to use with stems of heavy branches or shrubs, or flowers with small, weak stems.

In using the needle point holder, the heavy stems should be cut or pared at an angle on one side in such a way that they fit into the holder without breaking down the needle points. If the stems are not "sharpened" in this manner, often heavy branches will bend the needle points. Cutting the end of the stem in cross sections with clippers will soften it and aid in preparing stem for placement in needle point holder. Then

Clippers

press down on stem, bending stem in whatever direction is required by style of arrangement. (See sketch below)

Clippers

Clippers are a necessity and may be ordinary garden shears, strong, sharp scissors or the Japanese type of clippers. Obtain the Japanese type of clippers, if possible, since these are designed primarily for Japanese flower arranging.

Wire and String

Wire and string, neither too heavy nor too fine, are used to bind stems with sticks, to elongate stems by adding extra sticks, and generally to secure stems in the arrangement. Often a stick may be added to a stem in such a way that it is literally grafted. Wire is preferred for this work, but string may be used quite satisfactorily. In Japan, wet straw is used for this purpose, since flowers are usually purchased bound with straw. Up to the present time, all metals have been very scarce in Japan, hence the use of straw in place of wire.

Basket or Tin Box

A basket or tin box is useful to the arranger for storage of holders, shears, wire, string, extra sticks, etc., to keep equipment together and conveniently available.

| Cut One Side Of Stem End At Angle To Prevent Breaking Of Needle Points | Press Stem End Into Needle Holder, Then Bend Stem in Desired Direction |

Moribana style Form "A" with three pink roses combined with pittosporum leaves in a cream container, aqua lined.

Moribana style Form "A" using Liatris branches with loquat in a pale taupe container.

13

Moribana style Form "A" using peach-colored gladioli in a cream container, aqua lined.

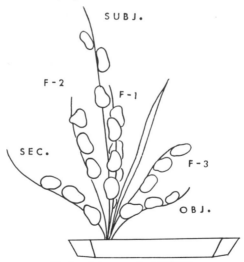

SUBJ.

F-2

F-1

SEC.

F-3

OBJ.

Study picture and duplicate,
following instructions on opposite page.

Lesson 1
Moribana Form "A" — Upright Style

The flowers chosen for this first lesson are gladioli, consequently their growing characteristic is strongly upright and suggests a Moribana Form "A" or Upright Style arrangement. Study the picture on the opposite page carefully, noting the positions of the stems and fillers when the arrangement is completed. The sketch below the picture illustrates the location of each stem and filler and will aid the student in preparing this arrangement.

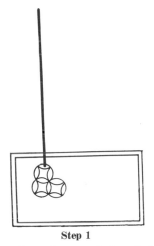

Step 1

The arranger has a low bowl or horizontal container, measuring, for the purposes of this lesson, 10 inches in length or diameter° and two inches deep. Whatever the dimensions are of the container used, follow basic measurement rule. Also at hand are an open type holder, string, clippers, etc.

Sketches which accompany the major steps clearly illustrate the appearance of the flower arrangement as it progresses toward completion.

Always prepare the material carefully, cutting away all dead and discolored leaves or faded blossoms and other superfluous material. Since we are using gladioli, cut off weak tips of the gladioli, especially if the flowers are very long. When flowers have been prepared, keep them in water to preserve their freshness so they will be as fresh looking as possible when the arrangement is finished.

Take the open type holder and place it in the container to the left rear, as in the form of an "L".

Select the best blossom, the one having the longest and strongest stem, measure the length, following Moribana style rule I which in this case gives us 10 inches, length of container, plus two inches, depth of

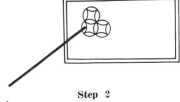

Step 2

° Diameter only if round container is used.

15

container, for a total length of 12 inches. Cut stem at this point and return to water. This is the subject which is kept in water until time to begin arrangement.

Select the next stem, this will be the secondary stem, cut it according to the basic measurement rule which is two-thirds length of the subject stem or eight inches in this case.

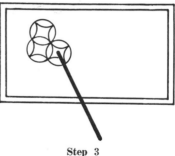

Step 3

Select the third stem, which will be the object stem, cut it according to basic measurement rule which is one-half length of subject stem or 6 inches in this case. Return to water after being cut.

The three remaining flowers are used as fillers. Cut filler 1 two-thirds length of the secondary stem. Cut filler 2 one-half length of secondary stem. Filler 3 is held in reserve until arrangement is completed, when it may be used to "fill in" any gap in the arrangement. This third filler is

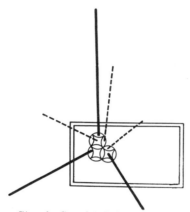

Step 4: Completed Arrangement

cut shorter or longer than filler 1, depending upon where it is used. Along with this third filler stem, leaves of the gladioli may be used to fill in and improve the arrangement, therefore, save trimmed-off leaves for this purpose.

Actually in Japanese flower arrangements, there would be no third filler, since florists in Japan sell flowers by the individual blossoms in assortments of odd numbers. Also, the Japanese use more foliage, shrubbery and relatively few flowers, as opposed to our American style which places more emphasis upon the flower.

Method of Wedging and Cutting Stems for Holder

With preliminary preparations and cutting of stems completed, we are now ready to place the flowers in the holder to complete the Moribana style Form "A."

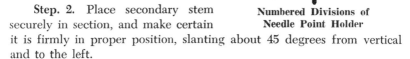

Numbered Divisions of Needle Point Holder

Step 1. Place subject stem in an upright position with bottom of stem resting in section. Make certain that stem is secure, and wedge it with short sticks or pieces of stem.

Step. 2. Place secondary stem securely in section, and make certain it is firmly in proper position, slanting about 45 degrees from vertical and to the left.

Step 3. Place object stem securely in section of holder at about an angle of 60 degrees from vertical. Slant stem to right front with blossom lower than secondary stem. Turn secondary and object stems slightly to center so blossoms show. Correct placement of these three principal stems is of paramount importance, since they form the design and framework for the completed arrangement.

Step 4. Place filler 1 adjacent to subject stem to fill out subject stem. Place filler 2 in rear partition, slanting filler to left or wherever it fits and looks best. Place filler 3 to right of subject stem slanting it right or wherever there is a bare spot to be filled in.

Add longest leaves of gladioli in back of stems, shorter leaves may be added in center of arrangement. These serve to trim up the arrangement. Often it may be necessary to remove principal stems or fillers to fit in leaves. If so, remove stems and supporting wedges, fit in leaves and replace stems firmly in proper position.

Finally, cover holder with bits of flowers, leaves, etc. Covering of the holder is comparatively new in Japanese flower arrangement and is the result of Western influence. It has been accepted as a real contribution to the art.

Use of Needle Point Holder

The same flowers and equipment, with the exception of the holder, that was used earlier in this lesson will now be used again. With the flowers already prepared and measured for proper length, place needle point holder in position in left rear of the container. Divide the needle point holder hypothetically into four numbered divisions as shown in the sketch on the previous page.

Step 1. Place subject stem in division 1 in an upright position.

Step 2. Place secondary stem in division 2 slanting to the left front.

Step 3. Place object stem in division 4 slanting to the right front.

Step 4. Place filler 1 in upright position to cover subject stem. Place filler 2 between subject and secondary stems, slanting slightly to the left. Place filler 3 between subject and object stems, slanting slightly to the right. Use green spears to fill out arrangement wherever appropriate.

Helpful Hints

Stems should always be cut under water. If possible have a small basin handy for this purpose. Also have a small amount of water in the container when placing flowers in the holder. Flowers, branches, shrubs, etc., should have their stems exposed to the air as little as possible, in order to remain fresh.

After an arrangement has been completed, leaves of branches, shrubs, and flowers may appear to be too dense. If so, cut out the excess, being careful not to trim out too much. In this respect, it will be helpful to cover the leaves, etc., with your hand before cutting out to visualize the final effect. Do not group flowers, branches, or shrubs too closely, keep the arrangement airy and let it "breathe".

Use seasonal prunings for branches or shrubs. Such materials may be obtained from a neighbor or your florist. All Japanese florists keep such material in stock and will sell branches and shrubs exactly like flowers.

When placing the stems in the partitions of sections of the open-type holder, hold the stem firmly in one hand, and have the small sticks to be used as wedges prepared and available for use. Take the free hand and place sticks around the base of the stem until it remains securely in the proper position.

NOTE: Roses, chrysanthemums, stock, spring and garden flowers or combinations may be substituted for the gladioli in Moribana style Form "A". These are easily obtained from your local florist.

Moribana style Form "B" using loquat branches with chrysanthemums in a cream container, aqua lined.

Moribana style Form "C" combining tritoma with tube roses and loquat leaves in a deep blue container.

Moribana style Form "C" with ligustrum branches and chrysanthemums in a white container.

19

Moribana style Form "B" combining yellow chyrsanthemums with pompoms in a cream container, aqua lined.

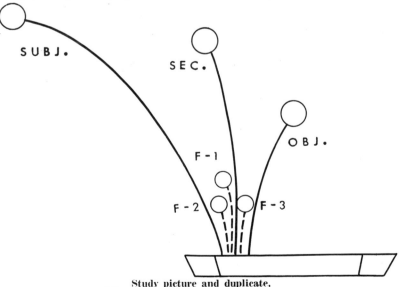

SUBJ.

SEC.

OBJ.

F-1

F-2   F-3

Study picture and duplicate,
following instructions on opposite page.

Lesson 2

Moribana Form "B"—Slanting Forward Style

This style is the second basic form in the Moribana type of arrangement and differs fundamentally from the style and form outlined in Lesson 1 in two respects:

a. The position of the holder, which is now placed off center to the left side of the container. Frequently in Form "B," the holder is placed close to the front, in this case it would be left front.

b. The slant or curve of the principal stem which is the major point of interest.

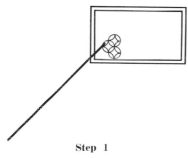

Step 1

Object of this type of arrangement is the position of the three principal stems as illustrated in the picture on the opposite page and the explanatory sketch below the picture, which shows clearly the exact position of each principal stem and filler. Chrysanthemums will be used in this lesson so that the student may duplicate the picture as closely as possible.

Same equipment as used previously will be used again for this lesson. Place holder in proper position in horizontal container as described above. Prepare flowers by removing dead and discolored leaves. Select the flower that will form the strongest slant, or has the best curve for subject, measure it according to Moribana style rule I, cut and place back in the water. Select secondary and object stems, measure them according to same measurement rule, cut and return to water to retain freshness. In this lesson, a few small pompom buds have been bound and tied together to act as fillers. With preliminary preparations out of the way, we are now ready to place the flowers in the container in the proper arrangement.

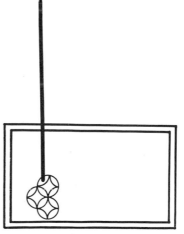

Step 2

21

Step 1. Place subject stem in small partition of section of holder, slanting it to the left front. If stem is too large, trim to fit partition; if too small, wedge securely with small sticks.

Step 2. Place secondary stem in small rear partition of section of holder, slanting slightly to the right rear.

Step 3. Place the object stem in section of holder, slanting low to the right front. With this third stem in proper position, the arrangement resembles a framework.

Step 3

Step 4. Place pompom buds fillers in center section of holder, between subject and object stems. Cover holder if necessary with leaves or other material.

Use of Needle Point Holder

Same flowers, equipment, etc., will be used with the needle point holders as we used above. With flowers already prepared, place holder in position off center at left side of container, towards the front, and begin to arrange flowers.

Step 1. Place subject stem in division 2, slanting or curving stem to left front.*

Step 2. Place secondary stem in division 1, slanting to right rear.

Step 3. Place object stem in division 4, slanting to the right in a low position.

Step 4. Buds may again be used as fillers and are cut and tied together and placed in the arrangement between the subject and object stems.

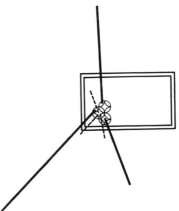

Step 4: Completed Arrangement

* See needle point holder diagram in Lesson 1.

22

Helpful Hints

In handling gladioli, chrysanthemums, etc., always hold the flowers with the blossoms facing upwards, never downwards. Also, do not cut stems of chrysanthemums, but instead break them.

Although the left hand side of the container has been used exclusively in these lessons, all arrangements may be made using the right-hand side of the container as well.

Whether the left or right hand side of the container is used depends upon where the finished arrangement will be placed. Always bear this in mind before deciding upon **any** arrangement!

These important facts must be considered and all are related to each arrangement:

1. Where the arrangement will be placed when finished.

Correct Way To Hold Stem

2. What container or vase will be used.

3. What flowers, branches or shrubs are most appropriate to use, considering both the type of container and final location of completed arrangement.

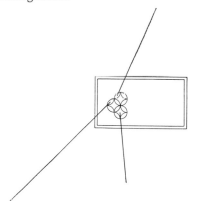

Never use more than three varieties of material in any arrangement. This prevents the arrangement from becoming too confusing and "fancy."

Although these arrangements are strictly devoid of any bunching of flowers as such, when the flowers are small, with weak, fragile stems, often they are tied together to appear as one flower.

When a branch or twig is cut, leaving a white spot, the Japanese rub a little earth on the spot.

Orthodox positions of ends of principal stems for Moribana Form "B" arrangement. See page 27 for detailed explanation.

NOTE: The selection of branches, shrubs, etc., is left to the discretion of the arranger, depending upon what may be obtained.

23

Moribana style Form "C" composed of pink roses in a cream container, aqua lined.

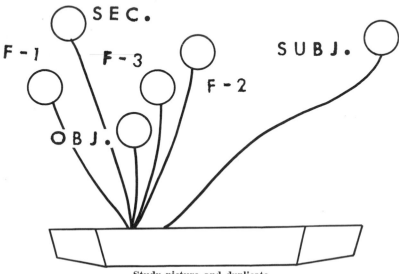

Study picture and duplicate,
following instructions on opposite page.

Lesson 3
Moribana Form "C"—Slanting Sideways Style

Form "C" is the final principal form in the Moribana style, and it differs from the first two forms in two respects:

a. The position of the holder in the container which is now placed at the left of center of the container;

b. According to the material available, the subject stem may have a strong slant or pronounced curve, so that when stem is placed in the container, the length of the stem will slant over the container. Because of the position of the holder, the stem will slant slightly to the front, as the arranger will discover.

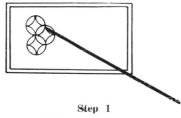

Step 1

The object of form "C" is to place the three principal stems in the positions shown in the picture on the opposite page and clearly outlined in the explanatory sketch just below the picture. As in the picture, roses will be used in this lesson. Equipment will be the same as used previously.

Place holder in proper position in container as described above. Prepare flowers and select one which may form a strong slant, or has a natural curve for the subject stem. Measure according to Rule I for Moribana arrangements and cut, placing back into water until used. Prepare secondary and object stems, as well as fillers, cut and return to water until used.

Step 1. Place subject stem in small rear partition of section of holder, slant stem to right front.

Step 2. Place secondary stem in small left partition of section of holder, slanting stem to left.

Step 3. Place object stem in small partition of section of holder, slanting stem to left front.

Step 4. Place filler 1 left of secondary stem, bending slightly to the left. Place filler 2 between secondary and subject stems, slanting to

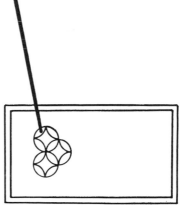

Step 2

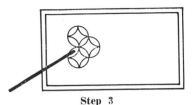

Step 3

the right. Place filler 3 in center in low position to fill in arrangement. Add additional leaves, ferns, etc., wherever necessary. Cover holders with rose leaves or other available material. Sometimes small rocks make attractive cover holders, serving both as a cover and also as a weight to hold down the holder should the arrangement become top-heavy.

Use of Needle Point Holder

Since the flowers are already prepared and cut to proper length, all that is necessary is to place the needle point holder in proper position in the container slightly off center.

Step 1. Place subject stem in division 3, slanting to right front.[*]

Step 2. Place secondary stem in division 1, slanting to left rear.

Step 3. Place object stem in division 2, slanting to the left front.

Step 4. Place filler 1 to left of secondary stem, bending it slightly to the left. Place filler 2 between secondary and subject stems, slanting to the right. Place filler 3 in the center in a low position, to fill in the arrangement. Add additional leaves, ferns, etc., and cover holder.

The student now has the essentials of the three major forms of low bowl arrangements. Remember that Form "A" used the subject stem in an upright position, Form "B" used the subject stem in a slanting forward style, and Form "C" used the subject stem with a pronounced sideways slant or natural curve.

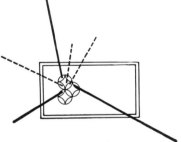

Step 4: Completed Arrangement

Students of flower arrangements should experiment with a variety of materials and combinations, always utilizing the fundamental principles of arrangement for the Moribana style.

Helpful Hints

In all Japanese arrangements, place the flowers in the holder in such a position that they appear to be growing from a single stem or root. This is a basic idea, both in the Moribana and the Heika styles.

* See needle point holder diagram in Lesson 1.

The dominant point in a Japanese arrangement is the subject flower or branch which is of paramount importance. In other words, the position of the subject stem is the key to and foundation of the style or design of the arrangement. Also, the Japanese do not use color wheels or charts. They study nature and add spice to their arrangements by attractive combinations of color, plus green leaves, etc.

Whenever possible, add greenery to any arrangement. This softens and improves the final picture. Just as cooking food without salt makes it tasteless and unpalatable, leaving green leaves, etc., out of flower arrangements, makes them "tasteless" to the eye.

The open type holder has many sections to be used. Use any of them for the fillers but keep the principal stems in the special partitions.

The diagrams illustrating the completed arrangements in the three Moribana lessons just completed are correct, but in order to impress upon the minds of the student the orthodox positions of the ends of the three principal stems, these additional diagrams are presented. It will be noted by observing the previous lessons that, although the flowers may be more vertical or horizontal, the **ENDS OF THE STEMS MUST BE PLACED IN THE CORRECT OPENINGS OF THE HOLDER AT ALL TIMES.** This forms the basis of simple Japanese Flower Arrangement. Identical positions are used in the needle point holder, despite the lack of openings.

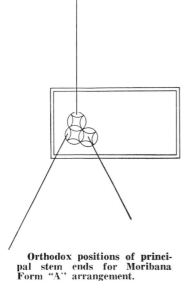

Orthodox positions of principal stem ends for Moribana Form "A" arrangement.

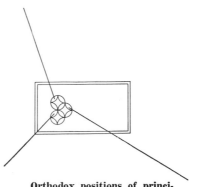

Orthodox positions of principal stem ends for Moribana Form "C" arrangement.

27

Moribana style Form D-1, Water Reflecting Style, combining spruce branches and small Spanish sabors with small daisy-type wild flowers in a pale blue container.

Moribana style Form D-2, Natural Scenery, using nandina branch with small cedar shrub and daisy-type wild flowers in a cream container, aqua lined. Holders are covered with rocks.

Lesson 4
Moribana Form "D"—Water Reflecting and Natural Scenery Style Arrangements

Strongly resembling and based upon the identical principles of Moribana style form "C" is the Water Reflecting style. Natural Scenery is based on Moribana Form A or B style of arrangements. Main idea for both styles is to depict in the container a nature scene beside either a lake or a stream.

Form D1—Water Reflecting Style

In the Water Reflecting style, chose either measurement rule I or II for Moribana style arrangement, depending upon the size of the container and the materials to be used. However, be certain that the branch used for the subject stem is very strong and resembles a miniature, overhanging tree and that the water in the container is much in evidence.

In regard to the secondary and object stems, these should be cut a bit shorter than the rule calls for, as they must in no way interfere with the dominance of the subject stem and the water in the container. Cover holder with small leaves, moss, rocks or whatever is available and suitable.

Form D2—Natural Scenery Style

Any of the principles that govern the Moribana styles may be used in the Natural Scenery arrangement. Moribana rules govern placement of stems, length of stems, etc. Main idea of this style is to depict a miniature version in the container of a woodland scene beside a stream or small pond.

There is one important difference between the Natural Scenery and the Water Reflecting styles. In the Natural Scenery arrangement, place the holder in one corner or part of the container and place your subject and secondary stems in that holder. If you have a second holder, then put it at the opposite corner or end of the container and place the object stem in this holder. This is a Moribana style Form A, modified.

As a result, you have small "embankments" on each side of the water, which now resembles a tiny stream or pond.

In both the Natural Scenery and Water Reflecting styles of arrangements, although the basic principles are observed, both arrangements draw vividly upon the imagination and skill of the arranger and both are very attractive and original forms of flower arrangements.

Lesson 5

Natural Versus Artificial Methods of Supporting Flowers

In using the horizontal container, the student has been placing flowers in fixed positions, using a holder. Naturally, if the flowers had been placed in the container without a holder, they would have fallen into the water or out of the container entirely.

Art. Meth. 1

Although Japanese flower arrangement in its broad sense dates back as far as the 6th century, it was not until many centuries later that the Japanese invented a holder for the low bowl type of arrangement. They already knew how to arrange flowers in the perpendicular vase, since that was the type of vessel in use for hundreds of years. Principal advantages of the upright vessel or vase is that the walls assist in keeping the flowers in the container, as well as the rim. Secondly, the Japanese devised methods of holding stems in fixed positions in the vase, using natural aids, such as the wall of the container, as well as props and wedges. These devices may be divided into two main types: natural and artificial.

Art. Meth. 2

Art. Meth. 4

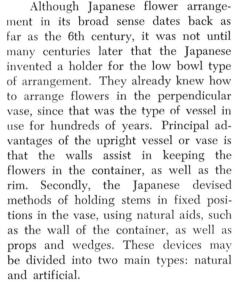

Natural Methods

Flowers, of course, can be placed in a vase and the stems themselves will hold the arrangement in place. For the sake of future reference, this will be designated as natural method 1.

Art. Meth. 5

Again depending on the stem for security of position, the arranger may cut stems of varying length and place them in the vase at an angle, fitting them snugly against the inner wall of the vase.

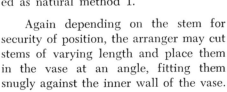

Art. Meth. 3

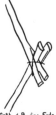

Meth. of Binding Ends

30

Art. Meth 6a

Art. Meth. 6b

Leaves and small flowers used to cover the mouth of the vase when arrangement is completed also tend to secure position of the stems. This is natural method 2.

The alternation of stems in the vase in various positions will lock stems into proper positions. This is natural method 3.

Stems are held in place by the rim of the vase which catches the ends of the stems, holding the stems securely. This is natural method 4. At all times, the stem is cut slant wise to insure a more secure fit against the vase wall—whether using the natural or artificial methods.

Art. Meth. 7-a

Art. Meth. 7b

Artificial Methods

Even with all of these natural methods, the arranger may find some difficulty in keeping certain stems in a given position. It is then that artificial means must be used. In addition to the methods described here, the arranger may devise his or her own. There is no corner on the market when it comes to artificial methods. Just make certain that it accomplishes the job and will hold the stem in the position you have chosen.

The same fundamental steps are always used in artificial methods.

Add. Art. Meth. B

Add. Art. Meth. C.

Art. Meth 6c

Add. Art. Meth. A

Artificial method 1: The arranger first measures the diameter of the vase on the outside and cuts a stick to this measurement, checking to see that it fits snugly inside the vase. If too long, snip small pieces from it, checking after each clipping so that too much will not be cut off. Bind this stick to the stem, branch or shrub and work stem and stick into the vase as far down as possible where stick will hold stem firmly in place.

Artificial method 2: Following the same procedure as in artificial method 1 for measuring, but rather than bind the stick to the outside of the stem, make a slit, 1½ inches or longer, in the bottom of the stem and insert the stick into this slit, binding securely. If the stem is weak, like that of a chrysanthemum or rose, split the stick instead and insert the stem into the stick, binding both together securely. Place stem and supporting stick into vase as described above.

Artificial method 3: Differs from methods 1 and 2 in that stem must remain long for balance, hence the stick to be inserted is slanted and placed low in vase.

Artificial method 4: This method differs from those just described in that a short stem is lengthened for balance. This length is gained by binding an additional stick to bottom of stem to lengthen stem. Then cut a second stick and insert it into this additional stick.

Artificial method 5: Differs in that a "Y" shaped stick is used, and both prongs aid in holding main stem securely.

Artificial method 6: Differs in that stem must remain upright and since stem is too short, an additional stick must be bound or spliced to bottom of stem. Measure stick from base of vase to end of stem. Cut stick slant wise, like a sharpened wedge, and insert into bottom of stem, binding securely. However, sometimes the stem will not remain in position. If this happens, the need of an additional stick requires the arranger to measure a stick across the base of the vase. This stick is inserted into the perpendicular stick previously bound to the stem. This added cross-stick is bound tightly with wire when necessary.

Artificial method 7: Provides two simple methods of using sticks, constantly employed by all schools of Japanese flower arranging, to anchor stems in place.

a. Place a stick directly across the inside of vase from one side to another. Fit the stick closely, otherwise, when water is poured into vase, the stick will float.

32

b. Place two sticks together in the form of a cross, tie tightly together and fit into vase.

Advantage of both these methods is that the stick forms a bar in the vase, which holds stems in position, and also provides a quick and simple solution. Other methods besides these described can be used. These methods are simple and the accompanying sketches will clearly show how to use them.

Best usage of these artificial methods comes with practice. For such exercises take a glass fruit jar and some flowers and sticks and use the methods described above. You will be able to see the exact position of the sticks, because of the glass sides of the jar, as well as the position of the stems when placed in such an arrangement and how the stems rest against the side walls of the vase.

NOTE: The number of flowers included in an arrangement is left to the discretion of the arranger. Often, more may be used, frequently less may be used. Number used depends on the arrangement to be created.

Heika style Form "A" combining magnolia
branches and chrysanthemums in a blue vase.

Lesson 6—Chrysanthemums

Heika style Form "A" using yellow
chrysanthemums with water oak leaves
in a deep blue vase.

Study picture and duplicate,
following instructions on opposite page.

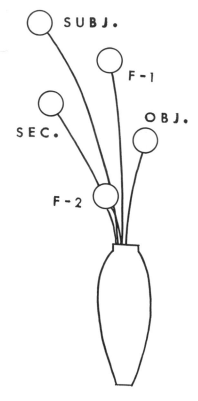

SUBJ.

F-1

OBJ.

SEC.

F-2

Lesson 6
Heika Form "A"—Upright Style

Now we arrive at the second major division of Japanese flower arrangement—the Heika (or Nagiere) style—which is intended for use in a perpendicular container or upright vase. The type of container differs, but the basic principles set forth earlier for the Moribana form arrangements remain constant and are used here. Nomenclature of stems and equipment will be the same, and only a few basic differences exist between the two styles of arrangement although the effect is varied.

In measuring principal stems for the Heika arrangement, remember that the subject stem measures $1\frac{1}{2}$ times the height of the vase. As in the Moribana style, the secondary stem measures two-thirds the length of the subject stem while the object stem is one-half the length of the subject stem.

Chrysanthemums will be used for this arrangement. Study carefully the picture on the opposite page and the accompanying explanatory sketch below the picture before beginning your arrangement.

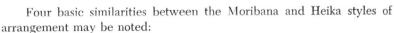

Step 1

Four basic similarities between the Moribana and Heika styles of arrangement may be noted:

a. The three basic and principal forms—"A", "B" and "C" are identical.

b. Names of subject, secondary and object stems, as well as fillers, are identical.

c. Each style requires that stems be placed in specific positions in containers.

d. Measurements are taken in almost an identical manner, and the ratio among the stems is identical.

Equipment used earlier will be utilized again, except that the container will now be an upright vase instead of a low horizontal bowl, and holders will be omitted. Otherwise,

Step 2

35

we have at hand clippers, wire, string, extra sticks for making use of artificial methods to secure stems in proper positions in vase and the flowers.

Following preliminary removal of dead and discolored leaves, and unnecessary twigs and branches, we are ready to select and measure the various chrysanthemum stems. Select longest and strongest stem, measure it against the height of vase, which for this lesson will be 10 inches in height. Add one-half of this height, or five inches for a total length of 15 inches for subject stem. The stem is marked at this point but NOT cut, since remainder of stem below mark must be below rim of vase in order to reach water and to be securely fastened in position. Return stem to water to retain freshness until ready for

Step 3

use. Although beginners will find it best to actually mark stem at proper height by using clippers, shears, etc., later on the arranger can remember correct heights without physically marking the stems. Measure secondary and object stems, mark but do not cut and return to water.

Select and measure filler stems, remembering that filler 1 is two-thirds length of secondary stem and filler 2 is one-half length of secondary stem, when measured above rim of vase. Filler 3 will be either long or short depending upon where it is to fit into final arrangement. In this lesson, water oak branches have been used to "fill out" the complete arrangement.

Step 1. Subject stem must be fitted into vase in an upright position, and it must remain firmly in position. Place in the left rear part of the vase. If subject stem does not hold firmly to its proper position, artificial means must be utilized to hold it in place.

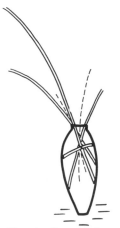

Step 4: Completed Arrangement

In this lesson, let us assume that the stem requires Artificial Method 1, as described in Lesson 5. Subject stem with stick is fitted into vase so that position is tight; leave end of subject stem long enough to reach the lower part of the inside of the vase. The stem then rests against the inside wall of vase for balance. Cut the end of the subject stem at an angle so that it will be able to rest against the inside wall. Stem now

36

stands toward the left rear.

Step 2. Place secondary stem in left front section of vase, slanting it to the left front.

Step 3. Object stem is now placed to right front of vase, slanting forward. This stem catches under the principal stem and its stick, or is placed wherever it may be secured. What happens to the stems below the rim of the vase is of no importance and their length is unimportant in that respect. Main thing is to be certain that stems are in proper position above rim of vase and will remain so.

When following lessons in this primer, the student must remember that she is at liberty to use whatever artificial method is necessary. In this lesson Artificial Method 1 has been used. However, because of differences in flower stems, branches, etc., another artificial method may be substituted to achieve the objective. Even original methods may be devised, depending upon the ingenuity of the student.

Step 4. Cut fillers and place them where needed, making certain they are also secured within vase. Cover mouth of vase with leaves or small flowers.

Important points to remember:

    a. Stems must remain firmly in proper position.

    b. Stems must be placed securely in vase.

    c. Stems must remain in water. Do not cut stems too short below rim of vase, so that they will be unable to reach the water.

    d. Fill vase with water absolutely to the rim.

Helpful Hints

For the beginner working in the Heika style, have long, strong twigs on hand, preferably fresh since they do not break too easily. These sticks are for use in any of the artificial methods, outlined in Lesson 5 for fastening supporting sticks to stems.

NOTE: Roses, snapdragons, poinsettias, calla and easter lilies and other strong-stemmed material may be substituted for the chrysanthemums in Heika style Form "A".

Heika style Form "B" combining white asters with leaves of nandina in deep blue vase.

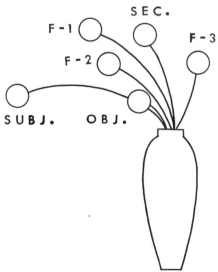

Study picture and duplicate,
following instructions on opposite page.

Lesson 7

Heika Form "B"—Slanting Forward

As we discovered earlier when planning a Moribana style Form "B" arrangement, the subject stem either slants forward or curves forward and is arranged to bring out these slanting forward characteristics. Heika style Form "B" follows the same form.*

In this lesson we will use asters. Study carefully the picture of a completed Heika Form "B" arrangement on the opposite page and the explanatory sketch which is directly below the picture. This is the exact arrangement we will try to duplicate in the instructions which follow. Stems and fillers are measured, using Basic Measurement Rule III, designed for Heika arrangements.

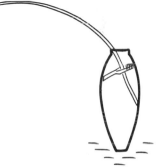

Step 1. Place subject stem in vase, slanting stem to left front. If stem will not remain securely in proper position, some means of artificial aid must be used. For this lesson we will use Artificial Method 2, in which the student makes a 1½-inch slit in the

Step 1

stick, inserts the stem into this slit and then binds the two together, as the accompanying sketch shows.

Step 2. Place secondary stem in vase, slanting to the left rear. Again, as for subject stem, some artificial means of support may be necessary to hold stem securely in place in vase.

Step 3. Place object stem low in vase, slanting slightly to the left front, making certain it remains securely in proper position.

Step 4. Cut fillers, placing them where needed. Cover mouth of vase with leaves.

* A forward style is necessarily very difficult to present properly in a photograph. However, the asters in the picture on the opposite page are slanting forward, although the vase has been turned slightly to the left, to clearly show the positions of the flowers.

Step 2

So far we have been using three fillers. As we progress and gain experience in flower arranging, we will find that additional fillers from blossoms, branches, and shrubs may be added with charming results which in no way detract, but rather add, to the beauty of the finished arrangement. In this lesson, one Nandina branch has been used to cover mouth of vase and to add softness to arrangement. After all, the object of flower arrangement is to create beauty!

It is important to remember, however, that the fillers must be cut shorter than the principal stems since the principal stems must remain the dominant feature of any arrangement. In this respect, fillers may be considered as spices and condiments, used primarily to season the dish.

Step 3

Helpful Hints

If the curve of the stem is slight and must be bent more, take the stem in both hands, bending it slightly a little at a time until the desired curve has been accomplished. If the stem or branch is too thick to bend easily in this manner, cut a small nick in it to aid the bending.

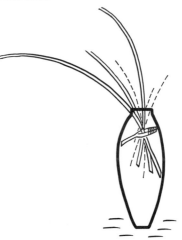

Step 4: Completed Arrangement

Be very careful and gentle. My Japanese teacher once remarked, "Well, even the monkeys fall from the trees." And even experts have trouble sometimes.

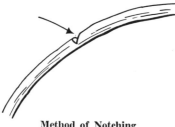

Method of Notching Branch To Aid In Bending

NOTE: Roses, carnations, snapdragons, lilies, or combinations, may be substituted for the asters in Heika style Form "B".

40

Heika style Form "C" using pine branches with sumac in a brown vase.

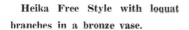
Heika Free Style with loquat branches in a bronze vase.

Heika style Form "B" combining persimmon branch with lavender chrysanthemums in a white vase.

Lesson 8—Chrysanthemums

**Heika style Form "C" using yellow chrysan-
themums with water oak in pale green vase.**

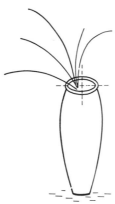

**Stems and fillers
confined to one-quart-
er of vase opening.**

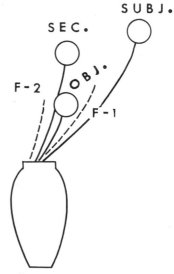

**Study picture and duplicate,
following instructions on opposite page.**

Lesson 8

Heika Form "C"—Slanting Sideways

The last of the six basic divisions of Japanese flower arrangements is the Heika style Form "C". The student will remember that this form employs as its subject stem a flower which forms a strong slant or broad sweep. If a straight stem is used, as was necessary in the picture on the opposite page, place stem in a slanting position. Study the picture carefully before proceeding with the arrangement. The sketch below the picture clearly depicts the relationship among and location of all stems and fillers. Chrysanthemums will be used, so that the finished arrangement may be made to duplicate that in the picture as closely as possible.

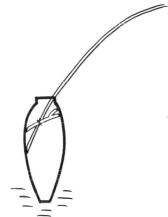

Step 1

As in the Moribana style, the subject stem curves or slants over the full height of the container, which raises the question of how to accomplish this, using a perpendicular vase instead of the horizontal container used in the Moribana style. As we progress with this lesson, we will see that the answer is really quite simple.

The principal stem is required to have a strong slant or broad curve, slightly horizontal. Measure stems and fillers exactly as in the previous lesson, remembering not to cut them until actually ready to begin making the arrangement. If stems need artificial support, experiment to determine which method will be best. In this lesson, we will use method 5 in which a "Y" shaped stick is used to support the main stem. However, the student may substitute whichever artificial method is suitable.

Step 1. Place subject stem in vase, slanting to the right of the vase, using artificial method 5 (or student's own choice) for adequate support.

Step 2. Place secondary stem in vase, to the left rear and slanting right.

Step 2

43

Step 3. Place object stem in vase at front, slanting to the right front.

Step 4. Cut fillers, placing them where needed. In this lesson, water oak branches have been used as fillers. Cover mouth of vase with leaves where necessary.

Step 3

Helpful Hints

All stems must appear to come from one section of the vase, no matter how spread out they may be in the final arrangement. This gives the arrangement a very neat appearance and can be accomplished even when heavy stems practically fill the mouth of the vase. (See sketch on page 42).

As a test to decide whether or not all stems are coming from one section of vase, divide top of vase with two sticks placed together in the form of a cross. If all the stems do not fit closely within one of the four sections, the arranger must continue to work.

As in the Moribana style, the finished arrangement may appear to be lop-sided. This is truly Japanese in design.

In making an arrangement of flowers, you are really creating a "picture." It has been my custom to place this "flower-picture" where it appears to the best advantage. If a picture on the wall interferes with the beauty of my "flower-picture", I merely remove the picture temporarily from the wall. This enables the observer to enjoy the "flower-picture" without interference.

According to the Japanese, the correct way to look at a flower arrangement is as follows: first look at the subject, then at the secondary and finally at the object. After looking at these three principal stems, view the arrangement as a whole and finally look at the container.

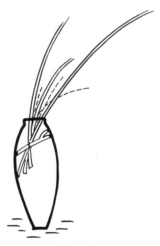

Step 4:
Completed Arrangement

NOTE: Roses, carnations, snapdragons, lilies or combinations may be substituted for the chrysanthemums in Heika style Form "C".

44

Moribana Free Style in a Natural Scenery using a moss-covered branch with orange colored pompoms and wild huckleberry leaves in a deep blue container.

Heika Free Style combining three pink roses with dried seed pod stems of palm tree in an oyster white vase.

Heika style Form "A" using cerise colored spider lilies in a lime colored vase.

Moribana Free Style of drift wood combined with green shrub leaves and crushed white shells on a black lacquer base.

Lesson 9—Pyracantha

Heika style Form "D" using pyracantha branch with bay leaves in deep blue vase.

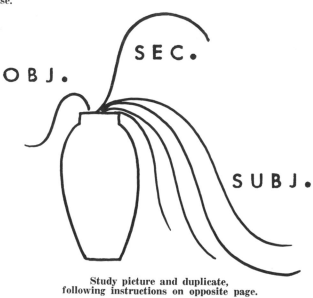

Study picture and duplicate,
following instructions on opposite page.

Lesson 9

Heika Form "D"—Cascade

Object of this style of flower arrangement, as its name depicts, is to have the principal stem or branch appear to fall from the vase in the form of a cascade. This arrangement should be placed, when finished, in a high position such as on a mantel, so that the branch may cascade down to its full length.

Select material appropriate for this type of arrangement. In this lesson, we will use a branch of the pyracantha. Great care must be taken in the selection of this principal stem since it must be long enough for Measurement Rule III and also have an additional small

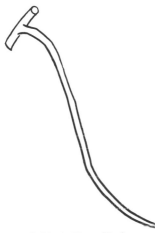

Subject Stem Hook

branch at its base which serves as a "hook".

Artificial Method 7a will be used to secure the principal stems in this cascade arrangement. This method utilizes a stick extending across the rim of the vase, under the lip of the vase, under which the main branch will be "hooked" firmly in proper position. This cross stick must be fitted tightly into the vase.

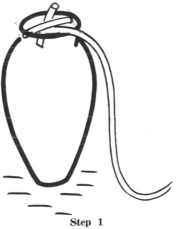

Step 1

Step 2

Prepare material in usual manner, discarding dead and discolored leaves, berries, and extra branches. Also prune additional material from subject

47

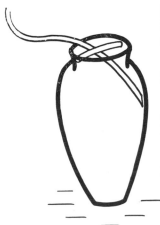

branch so that small branches will not interfere with the cascade appearance when completed.

Measure principal stems following Measurement Rule III.*

Step 1. Place subject stem under cross stick in vase, hooking it securely to this support.

Step 2. Place secondary stem in position, so that it stands upright but slanting slightly to the right.

Step 3. Place object stem at left front of vase.

Step 3

Step 4. No fillers have been used in this lesson, since the principal stems fill out the arrangement properly.

Helpful Hints

Japanese flower arrangement is based fundamentally upon the concept of a triangle. In all the basic styles or designs, if the arrangement has been correctly made, a triangle outline is very evident to the trained eye. In

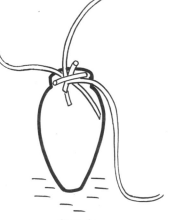

Step 4:
Completed Arrangement

order to help train the eye of beginner to recognize this triangle outline in Japanese flower arrangement, a very simple, yet practical, method is offered as a guide in this last helpful hint.

Take a string and extend it from the tip of the subject

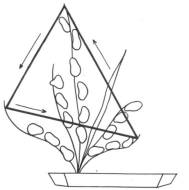

Triangle Outline
Using Moribana "A"
Arrangement

* Although following Measurement Rule III, secondary and object stems are necessarily shorter in order not to detract from subject branch in the Cascade arrangement.

48

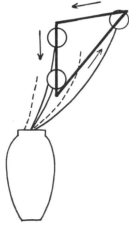

**Triangle Outline
Using Heika "C"
Arrangement**

flower, branch or shrub to the secondary tip, from the secondary tip to the object tip and back to the subject tip. If the string outline forms an asymmetrical triangle, it is correct in style and design, the stems are in proper proportion and the triangle is easy to visualize.*

Of course, in an actual arrangement, which is in three dimensions, the triangle is easy to see. In presenting the sketches, which are only two-dimensional, the problem becomes more difficult. However, in showing the Moribana style for "A" from Lesson 1 and the Heika style form "C" from this lesson, the triangle outline has been drawn. This will at least give the beginner the correct procedure for plotting this triangle. Do not be concerned too much about the fillers, unless they interfere excessively with the outline of the triangle. In that case, correct the arrangement by simply cutting them shorter.

Most all Japanese flower arrangements may be tested with the triangle outline method, except "free style." The latter is advanced, creative work, and exceptions are made to the rules in this case.

* This triangle used in Japanese flower arrangement is called an asymmetrical triangle which Webster defines as "want of symmetry."

Water Reflecting Style combining china berry branch with small, white daisy-type wild flowers and galax leaves in a yellow container pictured in a home.

49

Conclusion

Imagination, coupled with patience and practice, form the principal ingredients for the successful flower arranger. Beginners gain experience best through use of a wide assortment of materials in arrangements. Imagination will be the guide as to what to use and how to use it — within the bounds of the principles outlined in this book.

As in most art forms, it is practice that results in perfection. In Japan, the minimum course in flower arranging lasts three months. Even then the student has barely cracked the shell.

The author, working one day with her teacher, asked what period of time constituted a complete course in Japanese flower arranging. The teacher replied that the minimum course was one year.

It takes this long, the teacher explained, because the student must learn dexterity in handling flowers gently and must learn to train the eye in accuracy and correctness of design and style for each arrangement. Then, too, changing seasons usher in new flowers which the student must learn to use and combine in finished displays.

Thus, Japanese flower arrangement is not an art to be learned overnight, as we Westerners are so wont to do. Original arrangements are a corollary to a good foundation in this art.

Do not become discouraged too quickly and easily just because your first attempts at arranging flowers in the Japanese style are not successful. After all, it took the Japanese centuries to develop their technique and skills in this art.

Think constantly of Japanese flower arrangement while you are learning. Observe nature, let it be your guide. Notice the graceful curves and bends, how the flowers grow, etc. As I say constantly to my students, "Let the flowers and branches tell you how they should be arranged, let them be your guide."

Above all, enjoy yourself while you are learning the art. Let me assure you, the rewards, and they are plentiful, are there, but you must seek and strive to achieve them.

To quote Mr. Koshi Tsujii, another of the great masters of flower arrangement and with whom I studied the formal style, in a statement which I feel brings out the basic motive underlying Japanese flower arrangement: "The flower-vessel represents the good earth, and we should arrange flowers so as to make them appear as if they sprung from the earth and are still growing."

I can think of no better way to conclude this primer than to quote a tribute to the art of Japanese flower arrangement by F. F. Rockwell and Esther C. Grayson in their "Complete Book of Flower Arrangements." They describe the art by stating that "the creation of a good arrangement of flowers, based on the fundamental principles of design, blending with nature's rhythmic line and grace, can be an experience as enriching and satisfying as a fine picture."

An Historical Sketch of the Development of Japanese Flower Arrangement

Before commencing this historical sketch of the development of Japanese flower arrangement, it seems wise to have some knowledge of the character of the Japanese people. We all know that they are famous for their bold, strong, aggressive and fearless characteristics, but not many of us may know that they also possess the very antithesis of these traits, namely a deep-seated love of beauty, art, and cultural pursuits.

As far as history knows, the Japanese people are descended from a mixture of migrant Tartars from the north, and what apparently were Malayans from the south. The Tartar invasion resulted in inculcating the strong, bold characteristics, while the southern migration provided the love of art and culture.

Japanese flower arrangement had its primitive beginnings when the Buddhist religion was imported into Japan from China. The enthusiasm of Prince Shokoku for this new religion resulted in its being introduced to the Japanese people about 540 A.D. One of the early customs was to place flowers as offerings to Buddha in the temple.

Along with an increase in learning, art and culture, which were imported from China with the Buddhist religion, the civilization of the people advanced rapidly. The study and acquisition of culture was intensified and crude flower arrangements eventually developed into the magnificent creations for which Japan has become so renowned.

Creation of flower arrangements according to definite rules is generally credited to the Emperor Saga who originated it about 810 B.C. and authorities claim that he devised the system of Ikebana which, literally interpreted, means "flowers arranged according to rule." Therefore, the impetus to flower arrangement provided by the sponsorship of the early emperors and their followers resulted in such mastery in arranging flowers that it was eventually raised to the level of a fine art combined with a strong spiritual significance.

Another influence in the development of the art was provided by improved living conditions of the Japanese. In the centuries that followed, crude huts gave way to more elaborate and luxurious homes. Flowers began to be used for home decoration as well as for temple use. These floral displays were and still are placed in a Tokonoma — which is the place of honor in a Japanese home. This Tokonoma is a small recess in the wall of the home, with the base slightly higher than the floor, where scrolls, pictures, etc., are displayed.

From the emperors, noblemen, priests, etc., the technique of flower arrangement spread to other individuals gifted in the art and these laymen became the famous flower arrangement masters or experts in this field.

These early masters, by their continued efforts in the field, founded various schools. These original schools were forerunners of the present day schools in flower arrangement and this system has continued.

Each master has a great following, and there is considerable rivalry among the various schools in Japan, but the advantage is that the art is never dormant, and the intense spirit of competition has been instrumental in the development and progress of flower arrangement.

As the centuries passed, a love of flower arrangements became ingrained in all Japanese and it is rare today to find a Japanese who does not know something about the art. Flower arrangements are enjoyed by all from people living in the humblest homes and shops to those occupying the most luxurious homes and buildings.

In more recent centuries, the art of flower arrangement has developed and changed considerably, from a strictly formal syle to a more informal style, like the Heika (or Nagiere). Close contact with the Western civilizations has resulted in development of the Moribana style. It is interesting to note here in connection with the development of the flower arrangement art, that Mr. Ushin Ohara, founder of the Ohara School of Flower Arrangement and grandfather of the present master, Houn Ohara, about the end of the last century broke away from the traditional and formal style of flower arrangement. Today the art is following strictly modernistic trends, such as painting and sculpture have developed in our country and abroad in recent times.

At one period in the development of the art, it deteriorated because the rules became too numerous and rigid, and the beauty of the flowers appeared to be forgotten. But the Golden Age of flower arrangement (1573-1868) rescued the art and was responsible for its continued success.

The influence of the "tea ceremony," which was established prior to 1521, had a profound effect on the development of flower arrangement, particularly since the ritual required a floral display. Both religious sentiment and aesthetic feeling are harmoniously joined in these two cults. Japanese flower arrangement was not practiced solely for the satisfaction of arranging flowers beautifully according to the rules but because the art became imbued with a deep philosophical and religious significance. Thus developed a "way of life." In this connection, even the names of the principal stems were given religious significance and were known as Heaven, Earth, and Man.

Heaven is interpreted as being the "firm soul of all things;" Earth is "the source through which all things take form;" Man is "the fundamental way by which all things become active."

But we Westerners have accepted only the arrangement phase of the art. (I will add here, however, that though we have not accepted the philosophical and spiritual interpretations of the art, as outlined by the Japanese, whoever fails to rise above the "mundane" is missing much of its joy!)

This art has permeated Japanese life and is one of the noblest and most charming of pursuits. In its centuries of development, the Japanese have given to the world another art, an ancient one, but now modern. Regardless of when we live, Japanese flower arrangement has great appeal to everyone who loves flowers and is an art open to all.

Acknowledgements

I am grateful to the following persons who did so much to provide material assistance and encouragement in publishing this primer:

Editorial: Theodore E. Wasko.

Photography: Harry D. Dutchyshyn and Arthur Tubbs.

Illustrations: John Snyder.

Florists: Mr. and Mrs. Walter B. Murray of Murray's Florist, E. A. Botts of the Green Thumb, and Mr. and Mrs. James C. Bush of Bush's Florists, all of Augusta.

REFERENCES

Japanese Flower Arrangement by Houn Ohara, Master.

Mastery of Japanese Flower Arrangement by Koshi Tsujii, Master.

The Romance of Japan Through the Ages by James A. B. Scherer, Ph. D., LL.D.

Ikebana by Sofu Teshigahara, Master.

Modern Japanese Art of Flower Arrangement by Seika Nishizaka.

We Japanese by Atsuharu Sakai.

Representative Flower Arrangements by Koyo Maeda.